FOOTBALL SUPERSTARS

MBAPPÉ
RULES

SIMON MUGFORD   DAN GREEN

CONTENTS

MBAPPÉ! MBAPPÉ!

Kylian Mbappé is one of *THE MOST* exciting young footballers in the world.

The *super-fast* French forward is a

WORLD CUP WINNER

and an

AMAZING STRIKER.

WHAT MAKES **MBAPPÉ** SO FANTASTIC?

Let's find out!

Speed
One of the fastest players in the world.

Dribbling
Awesome at getting past defenders with the ball at his feet.

Tricks
Master of the fancy flick and super step overs.

Timing
Knows exactly when to make dangerous runs at his opponents.

GOALS!

OH YES – *MBAPPÉ* SCORES LOADS AND LOADS OF GOALS!

LET'S LOOK AT THE NUMBERS TO SEE WHY MBAPPÉ RULES.

3 ... 3 Ligue 1 titles

1 ... French Cup win

1 ... French League Cup win

81 ... goals for Paris Saint-Germain

1 ... **World Cup** win

13 ... goals for France

Estimated

£162 MILLION transfer fee

37 MILLION followers on Instagram

MBAPPÉ I.D.

NAME:
Kylian Mbappé Lottin

NICKNAME: *37*

DATE OF BIRTH:
20 December 1998

PLACE OF BIRTH:
Paris, France

HEIGHT: *1.78 m*

POSITION: *Forward*

CLUBS: *Monaco,
Paris Saint-Germain*

NATIONAL TEAM: *France*

LEFT OR RIGHT-FOOTED: *Right*

CHAPTER 2

BONDY BOY

13

1998 was a **BIG year** for **French** football.
In July, France beat **Brazil** in **Paris** to win
the **World Cup** for the first time.

Then in December, in the Paris suburb of **Bondy,** Kylian Mbappé was born.

Bondy is not like the **rich, famous** parts of **PARIS** with tourists, art galleries and museums.

16

MEET KYLIAN'S SPORTS-MAD FAMILY

Wilfried

His dad was a player and a coach at the local team, AS Bondy.

Fayza

His mum played handball in the French first division.

Ethan

Kylian's younger brother is a youth player at PSG.

Jirès Kembo Okoko

His adopted brother is a professional footballer, too!

Why was the footballer upset on their birthday?

Because they got a red card!

19

CHAPTER 3

FOOTBALL SCHOOL

Kylian **LOVED** football from the **first time** he kicked a ball. When his dad played and coached at **AS Bondy,** little Kylian would be there, listening to the team talks.

23

When he was six, Kylian was playing for Bondy's under-7s. Dribbling, passing, scoring - **Kylian was brilliant at them all.** He was the ***BEST PLAYER*** by far.

BOFF!

24

THE COACHES COULD NOT BELIEVE HOW GOOD HE WAS.

Kylian played in the under-11s when he was eight.

Kylian idolised players like **Thierry Henry** and **Lionel Messi**, but his favourite player was ...

Kylian wanted to be just like him, so he practised Ronaldo's **TRICKS, RUNS** and **GOALS!**

Kylian was 13 when he won a place at the famous French football academy, **Clairefontaine.** Players like **Nicolas Anelka, Olivier Giroud** and one of Kylian's heroes, **Thierry Henry** had all trained there.

WOW, this place is really posh!

Kylian trained on the amazing pitches at **Clairefontaine** during the week, but at weekends, he came home to play with his friends at **Bondy!**

WHO IS THAT KID? HE'S REALLY GOOD!

Kylian started to get his own **fans. Managers** from some **big clubs** came to see him play!

Some of the **BIGGEST** CLUBS in **Europe** wanted to sign Kylian.

He had a trial at **Chelsea,** but said,

NO, THANKS!

He even said **no thanks** to **REAL MADRID**, where he might have played with his hero

RONALDO!

"HE CAN BECOME AS GREAT AS **PELÉ, MARADONA** AND **MESSI.**"

Former PSG team-mate and legendary Italian goalkeeper, Gianluigi Buffon

34

Kylian did not want to live too far from his **family,** so he joined **Monaco** in **JULY 2013.**

He was **14 years old.**

PARIS

FRANCE

MONACO

Emmanuel Petit

Thierry Henry

Monaco had a great history. French World Cup-winners, like **Emmanuel Petit** and Kylian's hero **Thierry Henry** came through its youth academy.

COULD MBAPPÉ FOLLOW IN THEIR FOOTSTEPS?

Kylian made his **Ligue 1 debut** for Monaco, at home to **CAEN** in December 2015. Liverpool's **Fabinho** and Manchester City's **Bernardo Silva** were in the same team.

Kylian scored his **first goal** for Monaco two months later - a **93rd-minute** shot against **Troyes.**

GOoOOOO

MBAPPÉ VERSUS HENRY

MBAPPÉ

AGE AT DEBUT: **16 years, 347 days**

AGE DEBUT GOAL SCORED: **17 years 62 days**

APPEARANCES: **60**

GOALS: **27**

How does **Mbappé** compare to Monaco's previous teenage sensation – French icon

Thierry Henry?

HENRY

AGE AT DEBUT: **17 years, 15 days**

AGE DEBUT GOAL SCORED: **17 years 224 days**

APPEARANCES: **139**

GOALS: **28**

MONACO HIGHLIGHTS

SOME OF THE BIGGEST GAMES OF MBAPPÉ'S MONACO CAREER.

14 DECEMBER 2016

COUPE DE LA LIGUE, ROUND OF 16

Monaco 7-0 Rennes

Mbappé scored his first Monaco hat-trick in this thumping victory over Rennes.

11 FEBRUARY 2017

LIGUE 1

Monaco 5-0 FC Metz

Another hat-trick! Mbappe went on to score another eight goals in his next four league games.

19 APRIL 2017

CHAMPIONS LEAGUE QUARTER-FINAL, SECOND LEG

Monaco 3-1 Borussia Dortmund (6-3 agg)

Kylian's goal in this match was his fifth Champions League goal of the season!

MAN CITY MOMENT

15 MARCH 2017

CHAMPIONS LEAGUE LAST 16, SECOND LEG

Monaco 3-1 Manchester City (6-6 AGG)

44

Kylian scored his **first Champions League goal** in the first leg, but *MONACO* had lost **5-3**. Now they had to score lots of goals.

In the eighth minute, Bernardo Silva crossed the ball and . . . *BOINK!* Kylian was there to nutmeg the keeper.

GOAAALLLL!

Monaco went through on the away goals rule!

45

2016-17 was **Mbappé's** first full season for **Monaco.**

ALL COMPETITIONS RECORD

APPEARANCES	ASSISTS	GOALS
44	14	26

KYLIAN'S GOALS HELPED MONACO BECOME LIGUE 1 CHAMPIONS FOR THE FIRST TIME IN 17 YEARS.

CHAPTER 5

PARIS SAINT

47

Kylian's record at Monaco had made him **a star.** Europe's biggest clubs wanted to sign him.

This time, he said "NO THANKS!" to **Manchester City,** and "NO THANKS!" to **Real Madrid** – *AGAIN!*

He was a **Paris boy** - so it was

He went on loan to them in **August 2017**.

REAL MADRID HAD:

Karim **B**enzema, Gareth **B**ale
and **C**ristiano Ronaldo: **BBC**

Karim Benzema

Gareth Bale

Cristiano Ronaldo

BARCELONA USED TO HAVE:

Lionel **M**essi,
Luis **S**uárez
and **N**eymar:

MSN

Lionel Messi

Luis Suárez

Neymar

PSG HAD ALREADY BOUGHT NEYMAR FROM BARCELONA SO THEY HAD:

Kylian **M**bappé, Edinson **C**avani and **N**eymar:

MCN

Kylian Mbappé

Edinson Cavani

Neymar

PSG HAD A PLAN TO BECOME THE BIGGEST CLUB IN EUROPE.

The most expensive player in the world!

FIRST GAME, FIRST GOAL

8 SEPTEMBER 2017
FC Metz 1-5 Paris Saint-Germain

It was **Kylian's first game** for PSG. In the **59th minute,** a Metz defender cleared the ball straight to Kylian . . .

BOOM!

2017-18 HIGHLIGHTS

THE BEST OF MBAPPÉ'S FIRST SEASON AT PSG

12 SEPTEMBER 2017

CHAMPIONS LEAGUE GROUP STAGE

Celtic 0-5 PSG

Kylian's first European goal for PSG came in this Champions League thrashing of Celtic.

5 DECEMBER 2017

CHAMPIONS LEAGUE GROUP STAGE

Bayern Munich 3-1 PSG

Kylian was on the losing side, but he scored his TENTH Champions League goal.

Kylian became the youngest player to score ten Champions League goals!

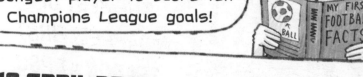

18 APRIL 2018

COUPE DE FRANCE SEMI-FINAL

Caen 1-3 PSG

Two goals from Kylian helped PSG reach the French Cup final, which they went on to win.

The more **goals** he scored, the more times Kylian could perform his **favourite goal celebration.**

Kylian **borrowed this celebration** from his brother **Ethan.** He did it when he would score a goal - *PLAYING FIFA!*

PSG TROPHY #1

31 MARCH 2018

COUPE DE LA LIGUE FINAL

STADE DE BORDEAUX

PSG 3-0 Monaco

Kylian won his first trophy with **PSG**

- THE FRENCH LEAGUE CUP -

against his old club!

He didn't score a

goal, but had **two**

assists and won

a **penalty**.

KYLIAN WAS MAN
OF THE MATCH!

TREBLE TIME

Paris Saint-Germain won **Ligue 1** with **five** games to go when they beat **MONACO 7-1!** They finished **13 points** ahead of Monaco.

RUB RUB

LIGUE 1 TROPHY

60

Kylian and his teammates ended the season by beating **LES HERBIERS 2-0** in the **COUPE DE FRANCE** final.

He had won an incredible **THREE** trophies in his first season!

COUPE DE FRANCE   COUPE DE LA LIGUE

2017-18

It was an **AWESOME** first season for **Kylian** at **PSG.**

APPEARANCES	ASSISTS	GOALS
44	21	15

He was voted *Ligue 1 Young Player of the Year!*

When **Mbappé** signed for

PARIS SAINT-GERMAIN

the fee was an estimated

£162 MILLION.

Kylian was the **MOST EXPENSIVE TEENAGE FOOTBALLER** in the world.

In 2018, Kylian appeared on the cover of the American magazine **TIME.** He was described as "the future of soccer."

They call football 'soccer' in America.

Lionel Messi, Neymar and
Mario Balotelli are the only other
players to appear on a **TIME** cover.

CHAPTER 7

WORLD CLASS

In 2016, Kylian played for **France** at his first international tournament - the **European Under-19 Championship.**

He scored against **Croatia** and the **Netherlands** before getting **two goals** and an assist to beat **Portugal** in the semi-final.

France went on to beat **Italy 4–0** in the final, which made Kylian a

EUROPEAN CHAMPION!

In 2017, France played in a **WORLD CUP** qualifying match. The finals would be held in Russia in the following year. **18-year-old** Kylian was called into the senior squad.

WHAT AN HONOUR!

His debut was against **Luxembourg,** and he scored his first goal against the **Netherlands.**

France won the group and were on their way to

THE WORLD CUP!

WORLD CUP 2018

21 JUNE 2018

WORLD CUP GROUP C

France 1-0 Peru

France faced **Peru** in their **second match** of the tournament. In the **34th minute,** Kylian picked up a deflected shot from **Olivier Giroud** and

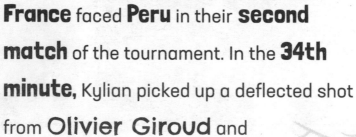

BOINK

- he had the ball in the back of the goal!

KYLIAN CELEBRATED WITH HIS FAVOURITE CELEBRATION!

Mbappé is the youngest ever French scorer at a World Cup.

He was 19 years, 183 days old!

France were up against **Lionel Messi's Argentina** in the **knockout round.** Kylian won a penalty which **Antoine Griezmann** scored, but shortly after half-time, France were **losing 2–1!**

Benjamin Pavard got them back to **2–2**, then it was Kylian's turn. He scored not one, but **TWO** awesome goals!

HIS TEAM-MATES WENT WILD.

LIONEL MESSI

Argentina pulled one back, but France went through and Kylian was

WORLD FAMOUS!

MBAPPÉ RULES!

WORLD CUP FINAL

15 JULY 2018

WORLD CUP FINAL

France 4-2 Croatia

The final was a crazy match! There was a
THUNDERSTORM, a dodgy **PENALTY,** an
OWN GOAL, a **GOALKEEPING
MISTAKE,** but importantly
for Kylian - he scored
a goal in the

WORLD CUP
FINAL!

80

FRANCE WON the tournament for the first time since **1998** – the year Kylian was born. Now, **at just 19,** he was a

WORLD CHAMPION!

MBAPPÊ VERSUS PELÊ

Kylian scored **FOUR** goals and won the
World Cup Best Young Player Award at
the **2018 World Cup.** He has been compared
to *PELÉ* – perhaps the best player of all time.

Kylian was the youngest French player to score at a **World Cup** and the youngest scorer in a final since **Pelé in 1958.**

WELCOME TO THE CLUB!

"WHAT HE CAN DO AT SUCH A YOUNG AGE IS NOT NORMAL ... THERE ARE A LOT OF KYLIANS, BUT ONLY ONE KYLIAN MBAPPÉ."

France manager, Didier Deschamps

84

CHAPTER 8

TOP BOY

At the start of the 2018-19

season for PSG, Kylian was given

a new squad number.

86

He was going to wear **NUMBER 7** - just like his hero **Cristiano Ronaldo.**

Kylian scored **_TWICE_** in his first game of the season - a **3=1** win over **Guingamp** in Ligue 1.

Then in the next game, **Mbappé,** **Cavani** and **Neymar,** each scored a goal in a **3-1** win over **Angers.**

MCN
WERE BACK!

LIGUE 1 2018-19 HIGHLIGHTS

7 OCTOBER 2018
PSG 5-0 Lyon

Kylian won a penalty, which Neymar scored, then went on to score **FOUR** *goals!*

What *have* you done to your hair?

I got some *highlights!*

19 JANUARY 2019
PSG 9-0 Guingamp

*Kylian and Cavani both scored **hat-tricks,** while Neymar netted two goals in this demolition!*

21 APRIL 2019
PSG 3-1 Monaco

*Kylian's third hat-trick of the season came against his old club **Monaco** and PSG were league champions.*

WONDER GOAL

Kylian scored one of his **best goals** of the season when he picked up a long ball from **Presnel Kimpembe** and -

BOoooOM

- he smashed it into the back of the net!

TOP SCORER

Kylian was the **top scorer** in **Ligue 1** that season, with **33 GOALS.** Across Europe, only **Lionel Messi** had a better league goal record that season!

Mbappé was the

LIGUE 1 PLAYER OF THE YEAR

and

YOUNG PLAYER OF THE YEAR 2018-19.

"KYLIAN HAS MUCH MORE TALENT THAN I HAVE. DO YOU SEE WHAT HE IS DOING AT HIS AGE? NO, I NEVER HAD HIS TALENT."

Paul Pogba

96

100 GOALS

In June 2019, Kylian scored for **France** in a **EURO 2020** qualifying game against **Andorra.**

BOFF!

IT WAS HIS 100TH PROFESSIONAL GOAL!

GOAL!

He was 20 years, 5 months old.

WHO WAS THE FASTEST TO *100 GOALS?*

NEYMAR
20 YEARS AND 1 MONTH
173 GAMES

MBAPPÉ
20 YEARS AND 5 MONTHS
180 GAMES

MBAPPÉ VS NEYMAR VS MESSI VS RONALDO

WHO'S BEST FOR THEIR CLUB IN ALL COMPETITIONS?

2016-17	GAMES	GOALS	ASSISTS
MBAPPÉ	44	26	11
NEYMAR	45	20	26
RONALDO	46	42	11
MESSI	52	54	16

2017-18	GAMES	GOALS	ASSISTS
MBAPPÉ	46	21	18
NEYMAR	30	28	16
RONALDO	44	44	8
MESSI	54	45	18

2018-19	GAMES	GOALS	ASSISTS
MBAPPÉ	43	39	17
NEYMAR	28	23	13
RONALDO	43	28	10
MESSI	50	51	22

FRANCE'S FINEST

Kylian has some way to go before before he catches up with the great French players.

But **winning the World Cup** at **19** is a **good start!**

KYLIAN MBAPPÉ
2017-

33
CAPS

13
GOALS

1
WORLD CUP

104

THIERRY HENRY *1997-2010*

123
CAPS

51
GOALS

1
WORLD CUP

1
EUROPEAN
CHAMPIONSHIP

MICHEL PLATINI
1976-1987

72
CAPS

41
GOALS

1
EUROPEAN
CHAMPIONSHIP

OLIVIER GIROUD
2011-

97
CAPS

39
GOALS

1
WORLD CUP

"WHEN KYLIAN DOES WHAT CRISTIANO DID IN MADRID – THINKING ONLY ABOUT SCORING – THEN HE WILL DO THE SAME. HE WILL BE SCORING 50 GOALS PER SEASON."

Antoine Griezmann

CHAPTER 10

BOY WONDER

HAT-TRICK HERO

22 OCTOBER 2019

CHAMPIONS LEAGUE GROUP STAGE

Club Brugge 0-5 PSG

Kylian had been out with an **injury** and started on the **bench.** He came on in the **52nd minute** and . . .

Scored with his **head . . .**

Assisted **Mauro Icardi** for a goal . . .

108

Scored with his **right foot . . .**

Then scored with his **left foot!**

In just over **20 minutes** he had scored his first *CHAMPIONS LEAGUE HAT-TRICK!*

CHAMPIONS LEAGUE GOALS SCORED AT THE AGE OF 20.

Kylian is the youngest player to score 15 Champions League goals.

	KYLIAN MBAPPÉ	*19 goals*
	KARIM BENZEMA	*12 goals*

	PATRICK KLUIVERT	*9 goals*
	RAÚL	*8 goals*
	**OBAFEMI MARTINS**	*8 goals*
	LIONEL MESSI	*8 goals*
	**JAVIER SAVIOLA**	*8 goals*
	**THIERRY HENRY**	*7 goals*

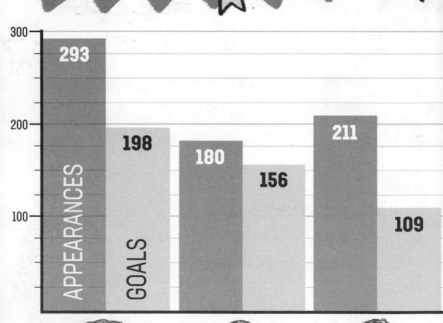

PARiS GREATS

300

293

200

198

APPEARANCES

180

156

211

GOALS

109

100

EDINSON CAVANI

ZLATAN IBRAHIMOVIĆ

PAULETA

112

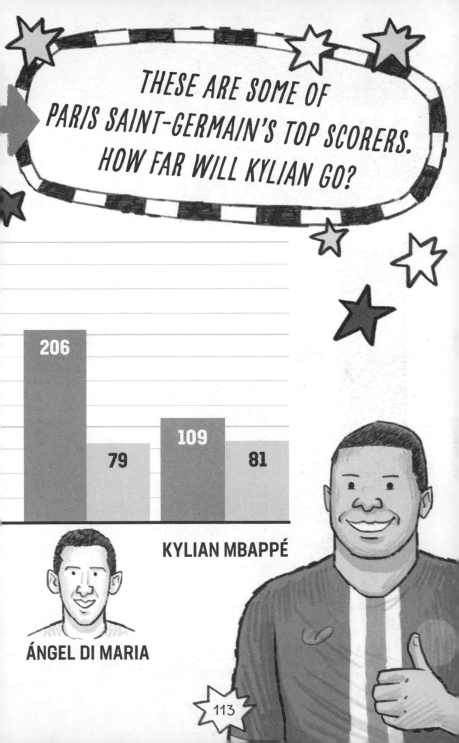

THESE ARE SOME OF PARIS SAINT-GERMAIN'S TOP SCORERS. HOW FAR WILL KYLIAN GO?

206

79

109

81

KYLIAN MBAPPÉ

ÁNGEL DI MARIA

The **REAL MADRID** manager **Zinedine Zidane** thinks Kylian is

AWESOME.

HE'D PROBABLY LIKE TO SIGN HIM FOR HIS TEAM!

In November 2019, he said:

"I'VE BEEN IN LOVE WITH HIM FOR A LONG, LONG TIME . . ."

CHAPTER 11

KING KYLIAN

Kylian donated **ALL** of his bonus for winning

the **World Cup** to **charity**.

He also gives the money he earns for each

France game to charities, too.

THANKS, KYLIAN!

Mbappé is one of the **FASTEST** players in football. He was recorded running at **38 km/h** in a game against **Monaco** in April 2019.

That's very fast! But not quite as fast as **USAIN BOLT** - the fastest man on the planet. He got up to **44.46 km/h.**

Usain Bolt

STEP OVER STAR

Kylian learned **tricks** like the step over by copying his **hero Ronaldo.** His opponent thinks he's going *one way . . .* but then goes **another way!**

HE RUNS HARD, THEN SWINGS ONE FOOT AROUND THE BALL.

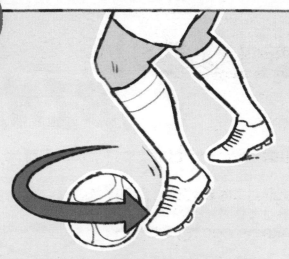

THEN SWINGS THE OTHER FOOT, THE SAME WAY VERY FAST!

AND GETS PAST THE DEFENDER – SEE YOU LATER!

TROPHY CABINET

Kylian has **won a lot** for such a **young footballer.**

LIGUE 1 WINNER
2016-17 (MONACO)
2017-18 (PSG)
2018-19 (PSG)

LIGUE 1 TOP SCORER
2018-19

COUPE DE FRANCE WINNER
2017-18

COUPE DE LA LIGUE WINNER
2017-18

TROPHÉE DES CHAMPIONS WINNER
2019

WORLD CUP WINNER
2018

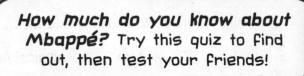

QUIZ TIME!

How much do you know about Mbappé? Try this quiz to find out, then test your friends!

1. Which local team did Kylian play for in his home town?

----

2. How many goals did Kylian score for Monaco in 2016-17?

----

3. Which American magazine described Mbappé as 'The Future of Football'?

----

4. Against which team did Kylian score his first European goal for PSG?

----

5. What does MCN stand for?

----

6. In which season did Mbappé win the domestic treble with PSG?

----

7. How many goals did Kylian score against Argentina in the 2018 World Cup?

----

8. Mbappé is the second-youngest player to score in a World Cup final. Who is the youngest?

----

9. Which squad number did Kylian take at PSG in 2018-19?

----

10. How many Champions League goals had Mbappé scored by the age of 20?

The answers are on the next page *but no peeking!*

ANSWERS

1. AS Bondy
2. 26
3. *Time*
4. Celtic
5. Mbappé Cavani Neymar

6. 2017-18
7. Two
8. Pelé
9. NO 7
10. 19

MBAPPÉ:
WORDS YOU NEED TO KNOW

Coupe de France
The top knockout cup competition in France.

Coupe de la Ligue
The second knockout football competition in France. The French League Cup.

Golden Boy
Award for the best player in Europe under 21.

Ligue 1
The top football league in France.

Trophée des Champions
Trophy awarded to the winner of a match between the Ligue 1 champions and the Coupe de France winners.

UEFA Champions League
European club competition held every year. The winner is the best team in Europe.

ABOUT THE AUTHORS

Simon's first job was at the Science Museum, making paper aeroplanes and blowing bubbles big enough for your dad to stand in. Since then he's written all sorts of books about the stuff he likes, from dinosaurs and rockets, to llamas, loud music and of course, football. Simon has supported Ipswich Town since they won the FA Cup in 1978 (it's true - look it up) and once sat next to Rio Ferdinand on a train. He lives in Kent with his wife and daughter, two tortoises and a cat.

Dan has drawn silly pictures since he could hold a crayon. Then he grew up and started making books about stuff like trucks, space, people's jobs, *Doctor Who* and *Star Wars*. Dan remembers Ipswich Town winning the FA cup but he didn't watch it because he was too busy making a Viking ship out of brown paper. As a result, he knows more about Vikings than football. Dan lives in Suffolk with his wife, son, daughter and a dog that takes him for very long walks.